Designed and produced by
Aladdin Books Ltd
70 Old Compton Street
London W1

Design   David West
Children's Book Design
Editorial Planning   Clark Robinson Limited
Editor   Bibby Whittaker
Researcher   Cecilia Weston-Baker
Illustrated by   Ron Hayward Associates

EDITORIAL PANEL
The author, Lionel Bender, is an
author, editor and producer of
children's illustrated general science
and natural history books.

The educational consultant, Peter
Thwaites, is Head of Geography at
Windlesham House School in
Sussex.

The editorial consultant, John Clark,
has contributed to many
information and reference books.

First published in the
United States in 1988 by
Gloucester Press
387 Park Avenue South
New York, NY 10016

ISBN 0-531-17092-2

Library of Congress Catalog
Card Number: 87-82894

INVERTEBRATES

LIONEL BENDER

GLOUCESTER PRESS
New York · London · Toronto · Sydney

CONTENTS

How the book works

Each section of the book describes a group of related animals. Each begins with an introduction and a large diagram of a typical animal from the group. Smaller diagrams explain the heart and blood circulation, and the structure of the animal's skeleton. Other pages have diagrams and color photographs that illustrate important points discussed in the text.

Throughout the book, charts provide a comparison of the forms and sizes of representative animals in a particular group. All illustrations are drawn to scale.

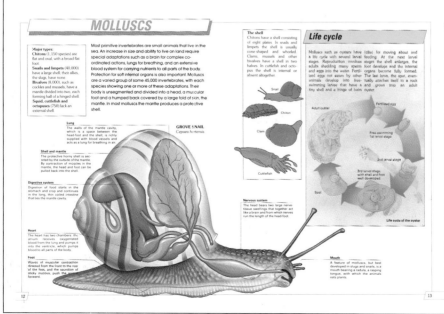

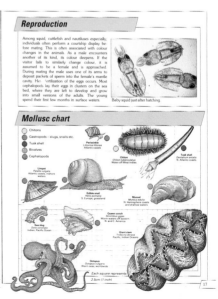

INTRODUCTION

Simple creatures – animals lacking a backbone – make up the vast majority of species on Earth. They have existed since its First Life forms evolved and have conquered every habitat – water, land and air. For example, there is no place on Earth that does not have some form of insect life.

Life first evolved in water and today the world's oceans and rivers teem with simple creatures. These range from microscopic single-celled creatures that float in surface waters as plankton to larger colonial animals such as corals and jellyfish. In the sea some soft-bodied animals developed a hard protective covering, such as shellfish. Others developed limbs and gave rise to today's crustaceans such as lobsters and shrimps. On land and in the air jointed-legged animals – arthropods – gave rise to insects and spiders. Only insects have developed the power of flight, and they remain the predominant life form on Earth.

This sea slug from the Red Sea is aptly named Spanish Dancer.

Single-celled animals are known as Protozoa. There are more than 30,000 species.
Major types:
Flagellates such as the pond animal called euglena.
Sarcodines, for instance amoeba, which moves and feeds using "false feet" (pseudopodia). **Ciliates**, such as the pond species paramecium, which is covered in tiny hairs called cilia. **Spore-forming** types, most of which are parasites, such as plasmodium.

All living things, from a tiny flea to a whale, are made up of microscopic cells. Cells are the building blocks of life, the smallest units of life that can exist on their own. Most living things are made up of many cells – they are multicellular. In such animals and plants, there are several different types of cells, each adapted for different jobs, for example nerve and muscle cells. Multicellular life-forms can each be thought of as an assembled machine. Their cells are grouped together to make various tissues, tissues combine to make organs, and all the organs combine to make up the complete animal. There are, however, many unicellular life-forms – animals and plants consisting of just one cell. These represent the simplest forms of life and were the first living things to evolve on Earth some 3,000 million years ago.

Animal cells

A typical single-celled animal is spherical or oval in shape and measures about 0.03mm (0.001in) across. In simple multicellular animals such as jellyfish, the cells are arranged as two layers – the inner endoderm and outer ectoderm. In between the layers is the jelly-like mesogloea. In higher multicellular animals there are three layers and the mesogloea is replaced by the central cell layer called the mesoderm.

Nucleus
Controlling the overall activity of the cell is the central nucleus. It contains the chromosomes, which are long strands of special chemicals that form a genetic blueprint of living things.

Cell membrane
The membrane is a soft, pliable skin which contains the cytoplasm and controls the flow of nutrients and waste products into and out of the cell.

Endoplasmic reticulum
This is a network of flattened sacs and tubes that form a communications link between the nucleus and the cell's surroundings.

Cytoplasm
Most of the cell consists of a watery fluid, the cytoplasm, in which all the structures are embedded.

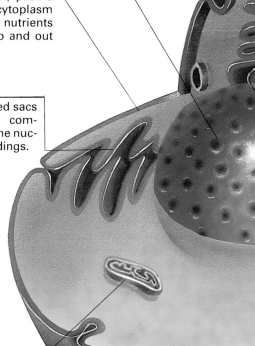

Two-layered

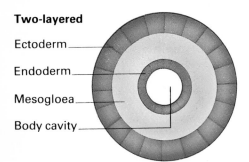

Ectoderm
Endoderm
Mesogloea
Body cavity

Three-layered

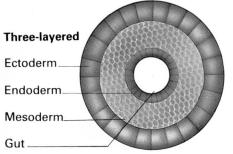

Ectoderm
Endoderm
Mesoderm
Gut

Mitochondrion
Energy needed for all the cell's activity is produced in the many oval-shaped mitochondria. They are the cell's powerhouses.

Feeding

Among single-celled animals, one group – the sarcodines – have a simple feeding action. This can be seen in the common pond animal, amoeba. When a piece of food comes in contact with the cell membrane, an amoeba pushes out a 'foot' that surrounds the food. With a pincer-like action, it engulfs the food and forms a vacuole or sac in the cytoplasm. Filling this with special chemicals, it digests the food.

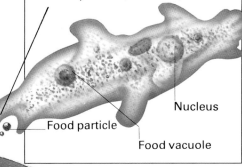

Pseudopodium (false foot)

Nucleus

Food particle

Food vacuole

TYPICAL ANIMAL CELL
× 5,000

Life cycle

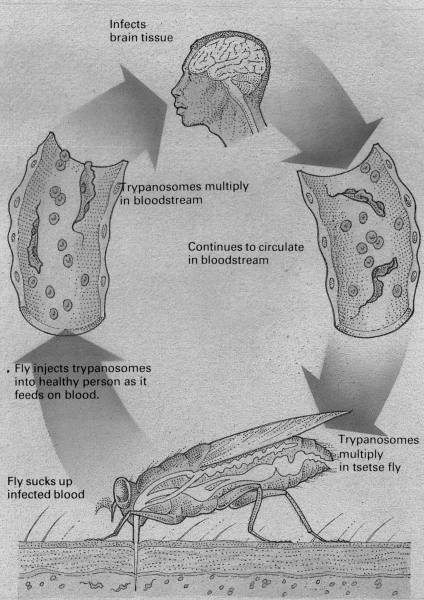

Infects brain tissue

Trypanosomes multiply in bloodstream

Continues to circulate in bloodstream

Fly injects trypanosomes into healthy person as it feeds on blood.

Trypanosomes multiply in tsetse fly

Fly sucks up infected blood

Single-celled protozoa, although simple in structure, have evolved a wide variety of lifestyles and are adapted to great extremes of availability of food. Many of them are parasites, depending on another animal, the host, for food. Some of these, such as the trypanosome parasite, cause diseases in humans. A species of trypanosome found in Africa has a life cycle involving two hosts, the tsetse fly and a human. It causes the human disease called sleeping sickness. The life cycle starts when the tsetse fly, the first host, feeds by chance on an infected person's blood. With its long pointed proboscis, or feeding tube, the fly pierces the skin to reach a blood vessel. It sucks up trypanosomes along with the blood. When the fly then feeds on a healthy person, the trypanosomes are transferred to a new human host. There they are carried around in the bloodstream to the brain, where they cause serious damage.

SPONGES, JELLYFISH, CORALS

Major types:
Sponges (over 5,000 species) include those animals with supporting spikes of chalk or silica, such as in glass sponges, or of soft spongin, as in bath sponges.
Jellyfish (200), sea anemones and corals (6,500) and hydroids (2,700), such as hydra.

Sponges are the simplest of multicellular animals. Each is just a two-layered bag of cells, with each cell working alone, engulfing and digesting food particles. Some of the cells form spikes that together give the animal support and shape. Jellyfish, corals and the related sea anemones also have a two-layered structure but groups of similar cells are arranged to form tissues, and groups of tissues make organs, structures that have a definite function. The two cell layers surround the hollow body cavity which is open at one end to form a mouth. Around the mouth are tentacles that draw water and food into the body cavity. Both sponges and jellyfish feed on other invertebrates and particles floating in the water.

Life cycle

Sponges, most corals, and sea anemones spend their life attached to rocks. They are often found in huge masses, as on tropical ocean reefs. Jellyfish are free to float in the water and are carried round oceans by the currents. Hydroids such as *Obelia* are small animals related to jellyfish that have a very complex life cycle with two totally different structural types: a slender, cylindrical, plant-like form, the polyp, which stays fixed to seaweed or rocks, and an umbrella-shaped free-swimming form, the medusa. The polyp grows and produces offshoots so that a colony of individuals forms. It also forms outgrowths which develop into medusae. As the medusae become fully formed, they break off the parent animal and float away. Each tiny medusa then produces sperm or eggs. The eggs are fertilized in the water and develop into hairy larvae, called planulae. These find a suitable resting place, and develop into new polyps.

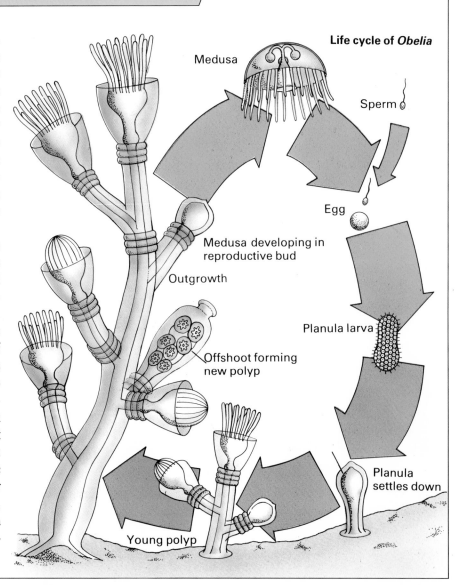

Life cycle of *Obelia*

Medusa

Sperm

Egg

Medusa developing in reproductive bud

Outgrowth

Planula larva

Offshoot forming new polyp

Planula settles down

Young polyp

Feeding

Sponges have special cells called collar cells which bear a long whip-like hair, a flagellum. By beating the flagella, the cells draw water and food particles into the body cavity. The tentacles of jellyfish, sea anemones and hydroids bear cells which capture live prey and are used to pull food to the mouth. Many of these animals have tiny plants – algae – living inside their bodies, and both benefit from the arrangement. Corals and anemones digest animal food and use the products for energy. Carbon dioxide is formed as a waste. The algae are plants and make use of photosynthesis, using sunlight as energy to combine carbon dioxide and water to form sugars. Oxygen is produced as a waste. Corals supply the algae with carbon dioxide, and the algae produce oxygen for the corals.

Sea anemones use tentacles to catch food.

Offense and defense

Jellyfish, such as the sea nettle and the Portuguese man-o'war, live in the sea and have trailing tentacles, some carrying stings. The largest type of jellyfish is 2.3 m (7.5 feet) across with tentacles 30 m (98 feet) long. The sting is produced by special cells and is used to stun and capture prey ranging in size from plankton to fish up to 30cm (12in) long. Hydroids and anemones are equipped with deadly weapons in the form of cells that act like spring-guns. Each cell consists of a tightly coiled thread wound into a capsule, with a trigger hair on the outside. When the prey swims against the trigger, the thread is shot out and snares the unsuspecting animal.

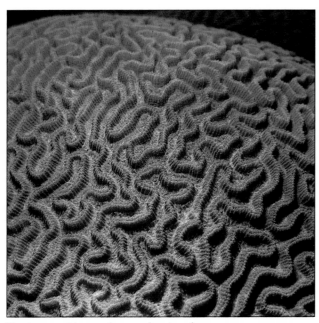

Brain coral is a colony of animals.

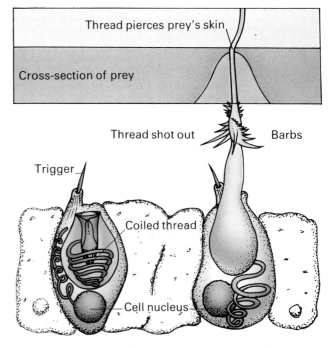

Thread pierces prey's skin

Cross-section of prey

Thread shot out   Barbs

Trigger

Coiled thread

Cell nucleus

WORMS

The name worm is commonly used for any long, thin, tubular invertebrate animal, but scientists distinguish many different types. The familiar earthworm and bloodsucking leech are segmented worms. Tapeworms, which people sometimes can get from eating undercooked meat containing their larvae, are parasitic flatworms, while the carnivorous *Planaria* (shown below) of ponds are free-living species. A parasite of sheep, the liver fluke, has a flattened body and does not look like a worm but is related to *Planaria*. Earthworms, instead of a cavity type gut, have a digestive tube with a front and back opening. Roundworms have an unsegmented body covered with a thick horny layer (cuticle).

Major types:
Flatworms – simple body plan, unsegmented – e.g. tapeworms (1,500 species), flukes (2,400).
Ribbon worms – unsegmented, covered in tiny hairs (750).
Roundworms – unsegmented, covered in a protective cuticle (over 10,000).
Segmented worms, the annelids, bristleworms (4,000), earthworms (2,500) and leeches (300).

Structure

The common feature of worms is a three-layered body plan. The middle layer of cells, the mesoderm, often has separate structures such as muscles and blood vessels. Flatworms such as *Planaria* show many of the characteristic features of worms. There is a distinct head region bearing the beginnings of a brain and sense organs such as eyes. The digestive system runs the length of the body and is branched to ensure that all parts receive digested food. Nerve cords extend from the head down each side of the body and allow coordinated actions. If the worm is cut in half, the head end grows a new "tail."

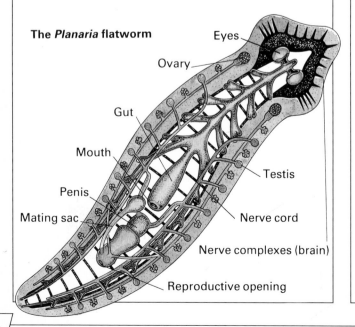

The *Planaria* flatworm
Eyes
Ovary
Gut
Mouth
Penis
Mating sac
Testis
Nerve cord
Nerve complexes (brain)
Reproductive opening

Mating

A host animal can rarely support two adult parasitic worms, making normal mating difficult. Such worms are hermaphrodites – adapted so that an individual's male cells, sperm, can fertilize its own female sex cells, the eggs. Most free-living worms such as earthworms are also hermaphrodite but the eggs of one worm must be fertilized by the sperm from another. At mating time two earthworms lie together head to tail and form slimy envelopes around their reproductive segments, exchanging eggs and sperm. The worms then separate and later each produces and deposits a series of sacs of fertilized eggs.

Earthworms lie together to mate.

Life cycle

Worms such as the tapeworm and liver fluke have a life cycle involving two different hosts and many developmental stages. The fluke, for example, lives as an adult in sheep. The worm produces fertilized eggs that pass out of this first host along with undigested food. Each egg develops into an immature form, a larva, that to survive must be eaten by the second host, a snail. In the snail, the larva multiplies and passes through other larval stages. Individuals of one such stage escape from the snail and form a protective coat around themselves. Only when eaten by a sheep will they change into the adult form. Although the worm's parasitic lifestyle requires being eaten by the right animal at the right time, its food is provided by the hosts.

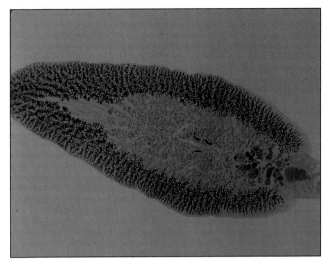

The liver fluke is a parasite of sheep and snails.

Feeding

Garden worms such as earthworms, and worms that live on sandy or muddy beaches, such as lugworms, swallow soil or sand and feed by digesting particles of animal and plant food contained in this. Most free-living flatworms engulf their food by enclosing it in the mouth-like opening to their gut. Feather worms, which burrow in the seabed, bear feathery gills that also act as food-collectors, directing plankton toward the mouth. Parasites in general have no need for an elaborate digestive system because all their food is pre-processed by the host. Some tapeworms have no real gut at all. They simply absorb nutrients through their body wall. The worm's cuticle protects it from the host's digestive juices, and it avoids being washed along the host's digestive system by means of suckers and hooks on its front portion.

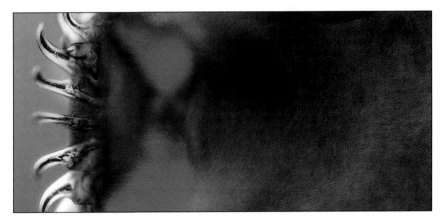

A tapeworm holds on using hooks on its head.

Lugworms leave casts near their burrows in the mud.

STARFISH AND SEA URCHINS

Starfish, sea urchins and their relatives are marine animals that form a group called echinoderms, which means spiny skinned. Beneath their outer surface is a rigid skeleton made up of plates of the chemical calcium carbonate (chalk). Often these plates bear spines that can be painful for an unwary swimmer. Echinoderms have no head, no true brain, and are unsegmented. The mouth is usually on the underside of the body. Unlike most animals, their body is built on a five-fold plan so that instead of only two sections of the body that are identical to one another, there are five. This body plan and lack of a brain limits their movements. All live in shallow or deep seas worldwide.

Major types:
Starfish (1,600 species) have between 5 and 40 arms and move using tube feet.
Brittle stars (2,000) move mostly using their arms not tube feet.
Sea urchins (800) lack arms and are spherical in shape.
Sea cucumbers (900) lack arms and are elongated.
Sea lilies (80) fixed on sea bed, and **Feather-stars** (540).

Structure

Starfish and brittle stars have five or more arms radiating from a central disk. The disk bears a water-filled ring canal and tube feet stick through holes in the skeletal plates. By means of water pressure in the canal system, the feet can be extended or retracted. At the tip of each foot is a sucker. Tube feet are used to collect food and for movement. Sea urchins and other echinoderms have similar tube feet or lack feet completely, instead using their arms for movement.

A five-armed brittle star

Feeding

Most starfish are meat-eaters. They prey upon shellfish such as scallops, prying open the shell with their tube feet. Brittle stars and most sea lilies and sea cucumbers feed on plankton and morsels of decaying matter. By beating the tiny hairs, cilia, covering their tube feet, they funnel the food to their mouth. Sea urchins have a diet consisting of both animal and plant food. Sea cucumbers living at great depths swallow sediment from the seabed and extract food from it.

A sea urchin's central mouth

A European starfish feeding on a bed of mussels

Life cycle

Echinoderms have amazing powers of regeneration – that is, if they lose part of the body a new part grows within a few days or weeks. Some starfish reproduce in this way, pulling themselves apart into several portions, each of which then grows into a complete animal. Generally, though, echinoderms reproduce sexually, with males releasing millions of sperm into the water and females releasing eggs. The fertilized eggs develop into free-swimming larvae that gradually grow into adults. Among some brittle stars, the fertilized eggs are kept within the female's body and the offspring are born as tiny replicas.

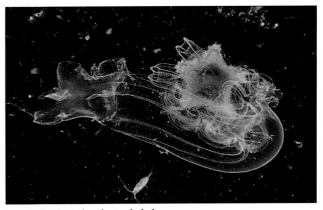

A newly hatched starfish larva

Primitive creatures chart

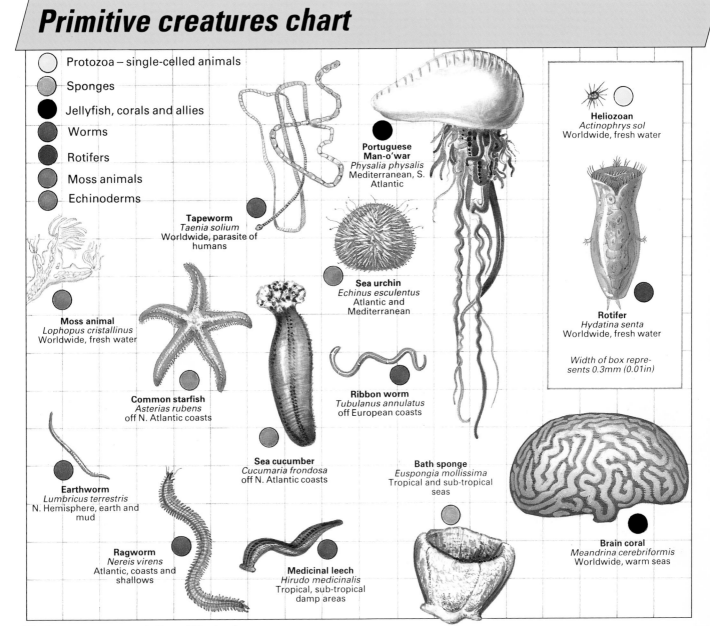

- Protozoa – single-celled animals
- Sponges
- Jellyfish, corals and allies
- Worms
- Rotifers
- Moss animals
- Echinoderms

Moss animal
Lophopus cristallinus
Worldwide, fresh water

Tapeworm
Taenia solium
Worldwide, parasite of humans

Common starfish
Asterias rubens
off N. Atlantic coasts

Earthworm
Lumbricus terrestris
N. Hemisphere, earth and mud

Ragworm
Nereis virens
Atlantic, coasts and shallows

Sea cucumber
Cucumaria frondosa
off N. Atlantic coasts

Medicinal leech
Hirudo medicinalis
Tropical, sub-tropical damp areas

Sea urchin
Echinus esculentus
Atlantic and Mediterranean

Ribbon worm
Tubulanus annulatus
off European coasts

Portuguese Man-o'war
Physalia physalis
Mediterranean, S. Atlantic

Bath sponge
Euspongia mollissima
Tropical and sub-tropical seas

Heliozoan
Actinophrys sol
Worldwide, fresh water

Rotifer
Hydatina senta
Worldwide, fresh water

Width of box represents 0.3mm (0.01in)

Brain coral
Meandrina cerebriformis
Worldwide, warm seas

Each square represents 5 cm (2 inches)

MOLLUSCS

Major types:
Chitons (1,150 species) are flat and oval, with a broad flat foot.
Snails and limpets (40,000) have a large shell; their allies, the slugs, have none.
Bivalves (8,000), such as cockles and mussels, have a mantle divided into two, each forming half of a hinged shell.
Squid, cuttlefish and octopuses (750) lack an external shell.

Most primitive invertebrates are small animals that live in the sea. An increase in size and ability to live on land require special adaptations such as a brain for complex coordinated actions, lungs for breathing, and an extensive blood system for carrying nutrients to all parts of the body. Protection for soft internal organs is also important. Molluscs are a varied group of some 50,000 invertebrates, with each species showing one or more of these adaptations. Although bivalves lack a head, molluscs' bodies are unsegmented and generally divided into a head, a muscular foot and a humped back covered by a large fold of skin, the mantle. In most molluscs the mantle produces a protective shell.

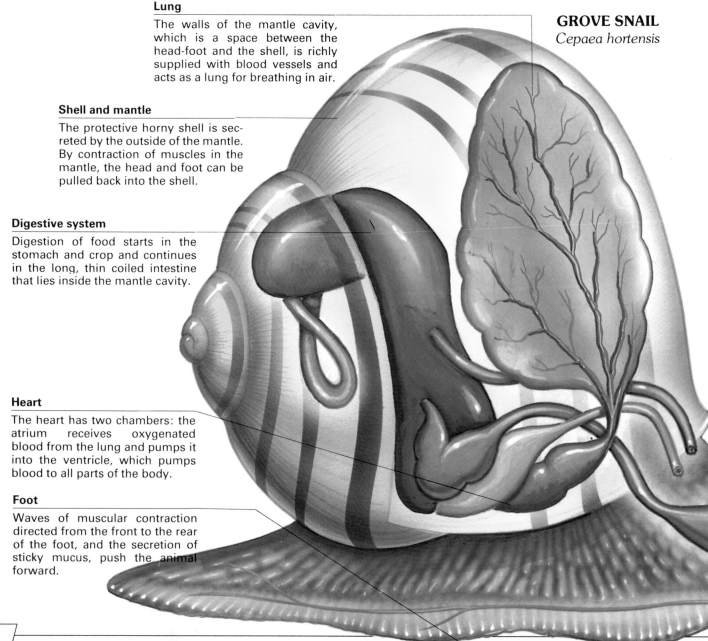

Lung
The walls of the mantle cavity, which is a space between the head-foot and the shell, is richly supplied with blood vessels and acts as a lung for breathing in air.

GROVE SNAIL
Cepaea hortensis

Shell and mantle
The protective horny shell is secreted by the outside of the mantle. By contraction of muscles in the mantle, the head and foot can be pulled back into the shell.

Digestive system
Digestion of food starts in the stomach and crop and continues in the long, thin coiled intestine that lies inside the mantle cavity.

Heart
The heart has two chambers: the atrium receives oxygenated blood from the lung and pumps it into the ventricle, which pumps blood to all parts of the body.

Foot
Waves of muscular contraction directed from the front to the rear of the foot, and the secretion of sticky mucus, push the animal forward.

The shell

Chitons have a shell consisting of eight plates. In snails and limpets the shell is usually cone-shaped and whorled. Clams, mussels and other bivalves have a shell in two halves. In cuttlefish and octopus the shell is internal or absent altogether.

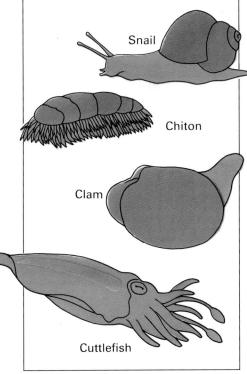

Snail

Chiton

Clam

Cuttlefish

Life cycle

Molluscs such as oysters have a life cycle with several larval stages. Reproduction involves adults shedding many sperm and eggs into the water. Fertilized eggs not eaten by other animals develop into free-swimming larvae that have a tiny shell and a fringe of hairs (cilia) for moving about and feeding. At the next larval stages the shell enlarges, the foot develops and the internal organs become fully formed. The last larva, the spat, eventually attaches itself to a rock and grows into an adult oyster.

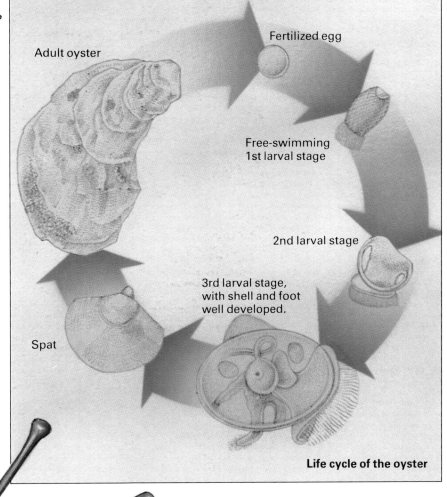

Fertilized egg

Adult oyster

Free-swimming
1st larval stage

2nd larval stage

3rd larval stage,
with shell and foot
well developed.

Spat

Life cycle of the oyster

Nervous system

The head bears two large nerve-tissue swellings that together act like a brain and from which nerves run the length of the head-foot.

Mouth

A feature of slugs and snails is a mouth bearing a radula, a rasping tongue, with which the animals eat plants or animals.

SNAILS AND BIVALVES

There are more than 8,000 species of bivalves and 40,000 species of snails and their allies, the limpets, slugs, sea hares and sea butterflies. They are distributed worldwide but mostly in temperate and warm seas and land areas.
Largest: giant clam of Indo-Pacific coral reefs – 135cm (54in) long and 330kg (730lb).
Smallest: coinshell, a bivalve, in the Atlantic – 0.5mm (0.02in)

Snails, slugs and limpets are the most successful of molluscs. There are species fully adapted to life in the sea, such as lovely colored tropical sea slugs. Different kinds of snails are found in gardens, ponds and lakes. Limpets and winkles inhabit seashores worldwide. Bivalves is a term often used for molluscs that have a shell divided into two halves and gills for breathing and for straining food particles from water. They inhabit estuaries and shallow waters. Some bivalves, such as razor shells, are burrowing animals, and others, for instance mussels, spend their lives attached to a firm base such as a rock. Bivalves include among others cockles, mussels, oysters and clams.

Feeding and breathing

Land snails and slugs breathe with lungs and feed by rasping at vegetable matter. Aquatic species breathe using gills that lie within the mantle cavity. Sea slugs lack a shell, and the gills are clearly visible as feathery structures on the top of the animal. Bivalves, too, breathe using gills. Water is drawn into the cavity via an inlet siphon or tube. Exchange of oxygen and carbon dioxide takes place between the water and the mollusc's blood. Used water moves out of the cavity through an outlet siphon. Bivalves are filter feeders, sifting food from water drawn in for breathing. The gills are covered with sticky mucus, which traps the food, and with cilia, which moves it towards the mouth. Siphons and gills can be seen between the halves of the shell.

A pond snail breathes using internal gills.

The outlet siphon of a cockle

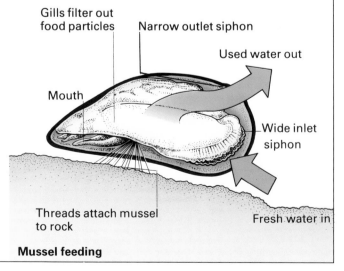

Gills filter out food particles
Narrow outlet siphon
Used water out
Mouth
Wide inlet siphon
Threads attach mussel to rock
Fresh water in

Mussel feeding

Mating

Molluscs such as the edible snail have both male and female sex organs. But mating is essential because an animal cannot fertilize its own eggs. Two snails come together and each shoots a chemical 'love dart' into the other's body. This stimulates the exchange of sperm between the two animals. The eggs are fertilized within the snails' bodies. After mating the snails move apart and each lays several batches of eggs in the soil or under stones. Some snails die after mating. The eggs hatch into tiny snails several weeks later. Among aquatic slugs and snails, most species reproduce like the land snail and release ribbons of fertilized eggs, but some shed their eggs and sperm into the water and fertilization happens there. Larvae hatch from the eggs.

Mating snails exchange sperm.

Movement

Sea hares and sea butterflies move by means of flat extensions of the foot that are used like paddles. Movement in limpets and most slugs and snails is produced by waves of contraction of the muscular foot. Bivalves such as clams and razor shells use their foot to burrow into sand. The foot is pushed into the sand, expanded to provide anchorage, then contracted to pull the animal downwards. This is achieved by forcing blood in and out of the foot and water in and out of the mantle cavity. Piddocks are bivalves that can burrow into rock, using their foot as a lever to move the shell to and fro and rasp against the surface to make a hollow. Scallops can propel themselves forward by opening the gap in the shell, the valve, and closing it quickly to force out a jet of water.

An Australian sea slug swims by body undulations.

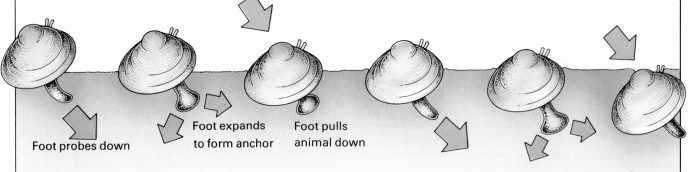

Foot probes down

Foot expands to form anchor

Foot pulls animal down

Clam burrowing into sand

Sequence repeated to burrow deeper

OCTOPUSES AND SQUID

Major types:
Squid and cuttlefish have a small internal shell.
Octopuses lack a shell.
Nautiluses are the only kinds with a complete external shell.
Cephalopods are marine animals of warm and temperate waters and include the largest known invertebrate, the giant deep sea squid, Architeuthis, which can be up to 18m (60ft) long.

The largest and most intelligent of all invertebrates are found among the cephalopods, a group of 700 or so molluscs that includes octopuses, squid and cuttlefish. Cephalopod means head-foot, and these animals have a well-developed head bearing a very efficient nerve complex – almost a true brain – and sense organs such as eyes and balancing organs. The head is surrounded by a circle of arms or sucker-bearing tentacles, which are modifications of the mollusc foot used for feeding. The foot is also adapted to form a muscular tube, the siphon, through which water enters and leaves the mantle cavity for gill breathing. This also provides the method of propulsion for cephalopods.

Swimming and hunting

Cephalopods move by jet propulsion, squirting water out of the mantle cavity through the siphon. Most octopuses, however, which spend their lives on the inshore seabed, crawl using their tentacles rather than swim. Cephalopods live as predators, feeding on fish, crustaceans and shellfish. Squid live in the open sea and cuttlefish on the seabed. Squid have eight tentacles, and a further two that are retractible and particularly long and used to seize prey. Octopuses have eight tentacles, which they wrap around their victims, and a poisonous bite. Nautiluses, which inhabit tropical waters, have many arms. Species such as the beautiful pearly nautilus have as many as 100, but they lack suckers.

A cuttlefish has a shell inside its body.

Suckered tentacles of a giant octopus

A nautilus moves by jet propulsion.

Reproduction

Among squid, cuttlefish and nautiluses especially, individuals often perform a courtship display before mating. This is often associated with color changes in the animals. As a male encounters another of its kind, its color deepens. If the visitor fails to similarly change color, it is assumed to be a female and is approached. During mating the male uses one of its arms to deposit packets of sperm into the female's mantle cavity. Here fertilization of the eggs occurs. Most cephalopods lay their eggs in clusters on the seabed, where they are left to develop and grow into small versions of the adults. The young spend their first few months in surface waters.

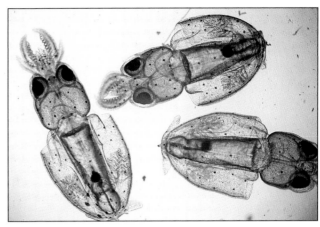

Baby squid just after hatching

Mollusc chart

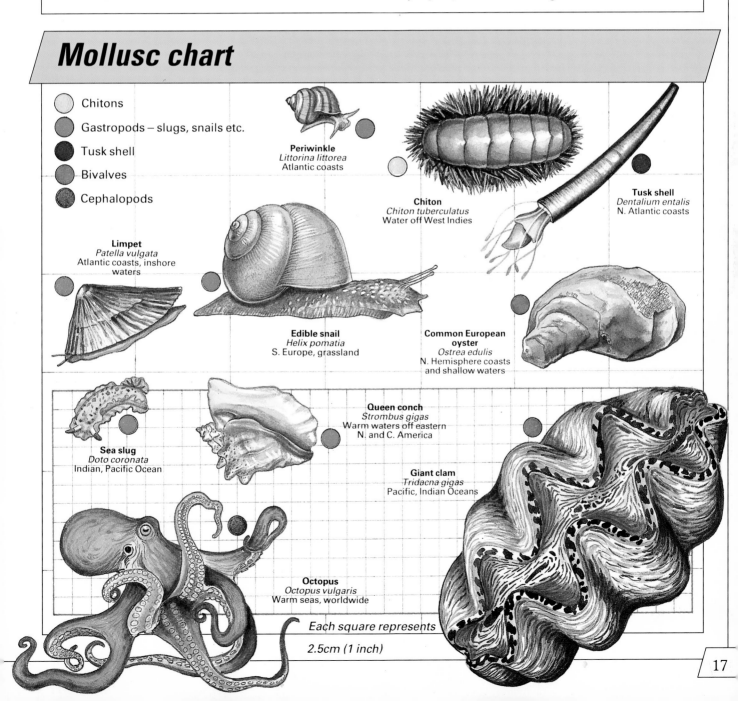

- Chitons
- Gastropods – slugs, snails etc.
- Tusk shell
- Bivalves
- Cephalopods

Periwinkle
Littorina littorea
Atlantic coasts

Chiton
Chiton tuberculatus
Water off West Indies

Tusk shell
Dentalium entalis
N. Atlantic coasts

Limpet
Patella vulgata
Atlantic coasts, inshore waters

Edible snail
Helix pomatia
S. Europe, grassland

Common European oyster
Ostrea edulis
N. Hemisphere coasts and shallow waters

Sea slug
Doto coronata
Indian, Pacific Ocean

Queen conch
Strombus gigas
Warm waters off eastern N. and C. America

Giant clam
Tridacna gigas
Pacific, Indian Oceans

Octopus
Octopus vulgaris
Warm seas, worldwide

Each square represents

2.5cm (1 inch)

17

ARTHROPODS

Major types:
Crustaceans, such as shrimps, crabs, lobsters, barnacles, woodlice (25,000 species).
King crabs (5).
Arachnids, including spiders, scorpions, mites (53,000).
Millipedes (8,000).
Centipedes (2,000).
Insects, including flies, dragonflies, cockroaches, ants, termites, beetles, lice, fleas and bees (800,000).

Arthropod means joint-legged, and most present-day kinds of these invertebrates evolved from earthworm-like animals that had a pair of limbs to each body segment. Four out of every five animals alive on Earth today are arthropods and they include insects, spiders, crabs, ticks and millipedes. They each have a body divided into a series of similar segments and encased in a horny layer, the cuticle. The cuticle is usually rigid and tough and forms an external protective covering, the exoskeleton. This thin tubular skeleton gives greater strength for its weight than a solid rod-like skeleton like humans'. Between them arthropods inhabit land, water and air throughout the world.

Breathing

Spiders, scorpions and many other land arthropods breathe through internal feathery gill-like structures called book-lungs. Species fully adapted to life in water, such as lobsters, crayfish and crabs, have internal gills like those of fish and draw water into the gill chamber where an exchange of oxygen (dissolved in the water) and waste carbon dioxide takes place. Insects have a system of tubes, the tracheae, through which air can circulate or, in some beetles, is actively pumped by air sacs near the spiracles. From the main tracheae, the air flows through smaller trachioles to muscles and organs. This breathing system is efficient but relies mainly on the free movement of air which is possible over short distances only. This limits the size of insects to only a few centimeters in length.

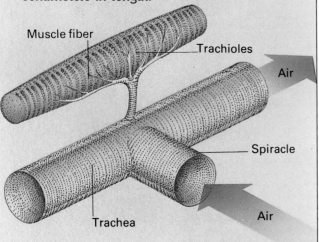

Muscle fiber
Trachioles
Air
Spiracle
Trachea
Air

Brain
A pair of nerve swellings, or ganglia, act as a brain and connect to the various sense organs. A nerve cord extends from the ganglia along the animal's lower surface.

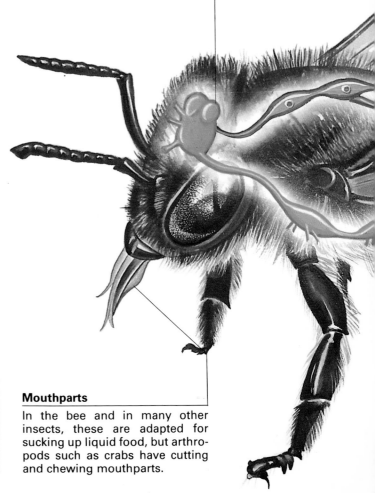

Mouthparts
In the bee and in many other insects, these are adapted for sucking up liquid food, but arthropods such as crabs have cutting and chewing mouthparts.

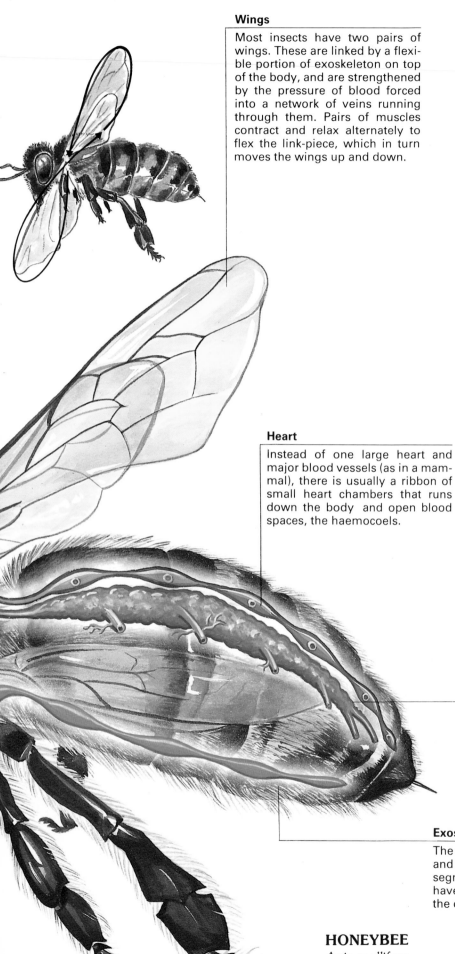

Wings

Most insects have two pairs of wings. These are linked by a flexible portion of exoskeleton on top of the body, and are strengthened by the pressure of blood forced into a network of veins running through them. Pairs of muscles contract and relax alternately to flex the link-piece, which in turn moves the wings up and down.

Body plan

Arthropods are bilaterally symmetrical – that is the left and right sides are identical. In addition, the body is divided into front, middle and hind portions. In the honey bee this is visible as the head, thorax and abdomen regions. In crustaceans such as crayfish, the head and thorax appear as a single unit, the cephalothorax. In insects, jointed limbs and wings are carried on segments of the thorax.

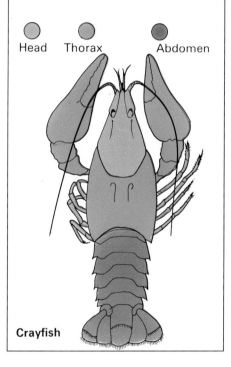

Head   Thorax   Abdomen

Crayfish

Heart

Instead of one large heart and major blood vessels (as in a mammal), there is usually a ribbon of small heart chambers that runs down the body and open blood spaces, the haemocoels.

Trachea

Air enters and leaves the body through holes on each side, the spiracles, and is pumped through an extensive system of tubes, the tracheae, to all parts. (See diagram opposite).

Exoskeleton

The internal organs are contained and protected within the tough segmented exoskeleton. Insects have a thick waterproof layer on the outside of the exoskeleton.

HONEYBEE
Apis mellifera

CRUSTACEANS

Major types:
Branchiopods (1,200 species), the freshwater shrimps and water fleas.
Copepods (4,500) are tiny aquatic species that form most of the animal plankton.
Barnacles (800), as adults, attach themselves to rocks, ships or other marine animals.
Shrimps, lobsters, crabs and woodlice (18,000).

Ranging in size from the 4m (13ft) span Japanese spider crab to tiny water fleas, and including lobsters, woodlice and barnacles, are a group of arthropods known as crustaceans. Most live in sea or fresh water and breathe through gills. Land species such as woodlice have specialized gills or breathe through the body surface, but this needs moisture and so the animals are confined to damp habitats. A typical crustacean, for example a lobster, has a large plate of skeleton, the carapace, over the thorax, and has a pair of legs or other appendages on each segment of its body. Its life cycle involves fertilized eggs that develop into larvae that are quite unlike the adults.

Feeding

Branchiopod, or gill-leg, crustaceans such as water fleas are filter feeders. By swinging their legs forward, they draw in water between them and filter off food particles. They then swing their legs back and this washes the food to their mouthpart limbs, which direct it into the mouth. Crabs and lobsters are scavengers, feeding on the remains of fish and marine animals. Their first pair of legs are adapted as nipping claws and their mouthparts are able to crush and chew chunks of animal food. Woodlice, or pill bugs, eat dead leaves and wood.

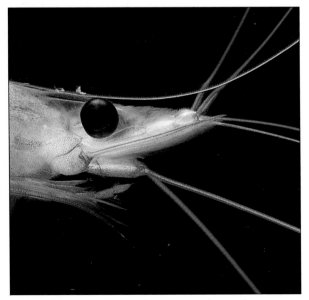
A deep-sea prawn feeds on particles in the water.

Growth

To grow bigger, an arthropod must shed its old exoskeleton and grow a new and larger one to replace it. During this period of molting the animal lacks support and is vulnerable to predators. When a crab is ready to molt, body tissues linked to the carapace break, and the animal hunches itself up and slowly withdraws, abdomen first. The new skeleton quickly hardens. This life-long ability to grow new tissues allows many crustaceans to regrow parts such as claws and mouthparts that have been injured or lost to enemies such as squid.

An edible crab shedding its shell

Life cycle

In most species the sexes are separate and individuals develop from eggs laid by the female following mating and fertilization. In aquatic species especially, fertilized eggs develop into a series of larvae. The first of these is similar in all species of crustaceans and is quite unlike the adults, with an oval body and three pairs of limbs. Freshwater branchiopods such as brine shrimps and water fleas produce heavily-shelled eggs that can withstand drought and cold. Pond water fleas can, in favorable conditions, produce offspring without fertilization of eggs.

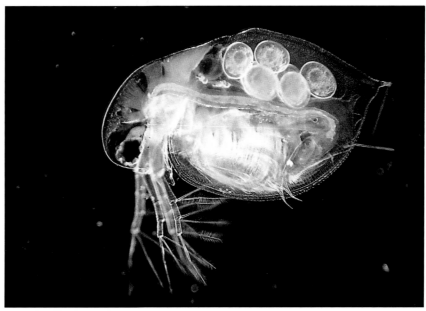
A water flea carries eggs inside its brood pouch.

Defense and protection

In addition to providing support, the exoskeleton gives arthropods varying degrees of defense against predators, parasites and disease-causing bacteria and viruses. The exoskeleton is composed largely of a carbohydrate, or sugar, type of chemical called chitin, but in crustaceans it is heavily impregnated with calcium salts for extra hardness. The carapace of lobsters and crabs is particularly strengthened in this way. In some land-living crustaceans such as woodlice, the armored exoskeleton is so jointed that the animal can roll itself up into a ball as protection against predators such as spiders. A waxy coating on the skeleton prevents water loss.

The mud lobster has a hard protective carapace.

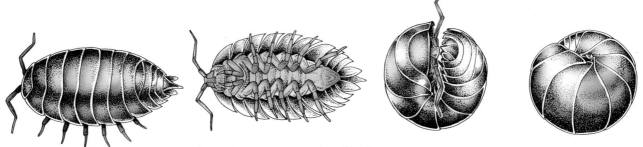
To protect itself the woodlouse rolls up into an armor plated ball.

ARACHNIDS AND KING CRABS

Spiders, scorpions and their relatives the ticks and mites (a group called arachnids), are probably the most disliked of arthropods because tropical species such as tarantulas have nasty poisonous bites, and many ticks, as skin parasites, produce unpleasant rashes and sometimes transmit deadly diseases. Most of these animals live on land, breathe using book-lungs, and are aggressive predators, preying on other small arthropods. Spiders, for example, are insects' greatest enemies. Unlike insects, they do not have antennae, and their mouthparts always include a pair of chelicerae, or fangs, that carry poison ducts, and pedipalps, or jaws. King crabs have walking legs and pincers like true crabs, but resemble spiders.

Structure

The basic plan of arachnids is a segmented body divided into two sections, a combined head and thorax, the cephalothorax, and the abdomen. The joint with the body is narrow like a neck. The specialized mouthparts are followed by four pairs of long, jointed walking legs. In spiders the rear of the abdomen bears six silk-producing glands, the spinnerets, and in scorpions it carries a poisonous spine used to paralyze prey. Arachnids have simple eyes rather than the complex, compound eyes of most insects, and do not rely greatly on vision to catch prey. But their sense organs do include hair-like projections of the cuticle that are sensitive to touch and vibrations. In aquatic species such as water spiders, these are also used to trap a film of air that is taken under water to a breathing bell of silk attached to water plants. This enables them to stay under water.

A female wolf spider

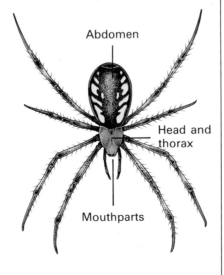

Abdomen

Head and thorax

Mouthparts

Parasites

There are many free-living ticks and mites that inhabit leaf litter and are involved in the breakdown of animal and plant remains in the soil. Most, though, are parasites and are found in large numbers on the surface of hosts that include fish, domestic animals and people. Ticks suck blood, and some mites hitch a lift on insects to move between food sources.

Harvestman infested with mites

Webs

Spiders that use silk to catch prey employ it as trip-wires, lassos or webs. Silk is spun as a thread from the spinnerets. Orb spiders produce a circular web and sit in the middle of this waiting for an insect to get caught in sticky drops on the threads. As the first stage in making the web, the spider spins a long thread which will then be blown by the wind to a nearby support (1). Having made this bridge thread, it crosses it, lays down a second thread (2), then pulls this into a V-shape (3). With the frame complete, the spider adds arms, or radii, to make a platform in the middle (4). It then forms spiral threads (5) and completes the web (6).

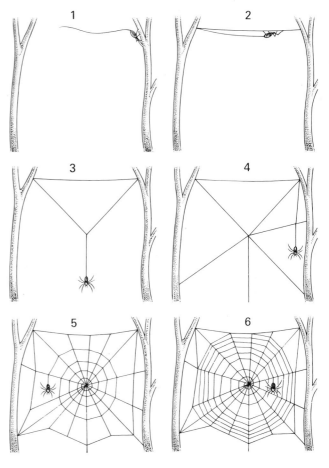

An orb spider wrapping its prey in silk

Breathing

King crabs live on or near shores of North America and much of Southeast Asia. Like spiders, scorpions and most other arachnids, they breathe through book-lungs. In spiders these are gill-like structures made up of leaves, like the pages of a book, each containing circulating blood and in contact with air drawn into the lung chamber. King crabs have five pairs of book-lungs, each consisting of as many as 200 thin leaves. They are adapted for breathing in water so whenever these arthropods come out to the beach, as they do to breed, they must keep the book-lungs moist. This they do by plowing along in the sand. In the water, king crabs swim along upside down flapping the book-lungs, an action that circulates water among the lung leaves.

A king crab has six pairs of limbs.

Feeding

Most arachnids feed on animal food, which they can only take in liquid form. They must therefore kill or stun their prey then pump it full of digestive juices before sucking out the semi-digested contents. Scorpions are limited to the warm regions of the world. They feed mainly at night, capturing insects with their pincers then using their sting to poison or paralyze the prey. Harvestmen, which look like long-legged spiders, live in low-growing vegetation and as well as hunting small invertebrates, also eat dead animal and plant material. Parasitic ticks and mites have mouthparts adapted for piercing and clinging to the host's outer surface and for sucking up blood or, in the case of plant parasites, sap. Most do not kill their host unless they infect them with germs that they carry. Among spiders, many construct webs to trap flying insects. The web may be circular and elegantly built, funnel-shaped, or just a formless tangle of silk threads. Raft spiders hunt on water by detecting surface vibrations made by insects such as mosquitoes. Tropical trapdoor spiders live in an underground burrow and as an insect passes by, flap open the hinged cover of the burrow and pounce. Wolf spiders chase prey, and jumping spiders stalk and pounce. South American tarantulas, or bird-eating spiders, prey on small birds and reptiles but usually eat invertebrates. King crabs gather small worms and shellfish from the seabed.

An Australian scorpion killing a cricket

A trapdoor spider emerges from its lair

A water spider with a dead fly in its 'larder'

Mating

Spiders have the most elaborate mating system among arachnids. The male spins a small web, deposits its sperm on it, then sucks up the sperm into special storage organs near its mouth. He then goes in search of a mate. The male courts the female in one of many ways. He may use a visual display, waving his legs about to signal he carries sperm. Or he may touch her, present her with food gift wrapped in silk, or vibrate her web in a special way. During mating the male inserts his pedipalps into the female's sperm-storing organs and deposits sufficient sperm to fertilize several batches of eggs. After mating the male often dies, usually through exhaustion although female black widow spiders of North America devour their mate, which is much smaller in size.

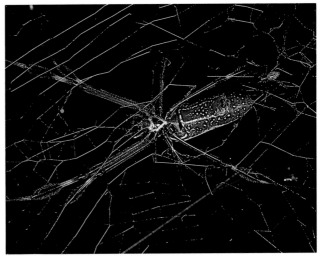

A female spider and her tiny mate

Offspring

Female spiders lay several batches of eggs each year and enclose each batch with a silken cocoon or covering. The common European garden spider, for example, may lay ten batches of 1,000 or more eggs each. The cocoons can often be seen on garden plants in late summer. Some female spiders bury the cocoons in soil and leave the offspring to fend for themselves. Several tropical species guard the eggs from insect predators or, as in wolf spiders, carry them around on their back. Young spiderlings hatch in the cocoons and a few days later emerge. They allow themselves to be dispersed by the wind. They then go through several molts before reaching adult size and acquiring fully formed eyes, spinnerets and claws on their legs. Scorpions produce large numbers of live young, which the female initially carries around on her back.

A mother scorpion carrying her 28 babies

INSECTS

Numbering more than 800,000 species, insects have colonized the world more widely than any other group of animals. They are absent only from deep sea water. Some, such as fleas and lice, are parasites of mammals. Desert locusts are major pests of crops, and tropical mosquitoes carry diseases such as malaria. High-flying species form an aerial plankton on which many birds depend for food. As arthropods, they have a segmented, three-section body. The head bears specialized sense organs, the antennae, and the thorax has three pairs of walking legs and usually two pairs of wings. The abdomen often has jointed structures adapted for mating or stinging.

Life cycle

Insects can be divided into two distinct groups based on the type of offspring that emerge from the females' fertilized eggs. Among wingless insects and the most primitive winged species, such as earwigs and locusts, the eggs hatch into young that closely resemble the adults. The young are often called nymphs. All other insects produce eggs that hatch into larvae, which are quite unlike the adults and usually feed on entirely different food. A female gnat, for example, lays eggs as a raft on water. After a few days these hatch into larvae that breathe air at the surface through special tracheal tubes and feed on microscopic algae in the water. Each larva then changes into a pre-adult stage, the pupa. This too breathes air but does not feed. Finally, the pupal skin splits open and the young adult, flying insect emerges, and the cycle continues. Adult male gnats feed on nectar, and females on the blood of birds or small mammals.

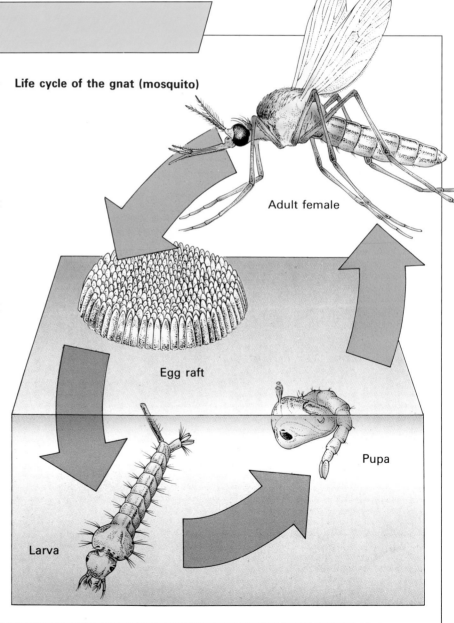

Life cycle of the gnat (mosquito)

Adult female

Egg raft

Larva

Pupa

Flying

True flies, called dipterans, have just one pair of flying wings. So too do cockroaches and beetles and their allies, the cockchafers and ladybirds, although they also have a pair of non-flying wings that are modified to form protective wing covers, the elytra. Species with two pairs of flying wings include butterflies and moths, mayflies, and dragonflies. Some dragonflies can fly at speeds of 100 kph (65mph).

A seven-spot ladybird flying to a flower

Jumping

Springtails have a special forked structure on their abdomen that acts like a spring and enables them to jump. Fleas, crickets and grasshoppers jump by folding up then quickly extending their long powerful hindlegs. Fleas can jump more than 30cm (12in) high. As wingless insects, this is an adaptation to their way of life. Female fleas lay their eggs on the ground, and the adults that develop from the larvae have to be able to leap in the air to attach to a host animal.

Flea

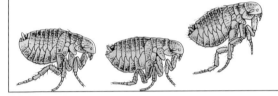

Walking and swimming

Aquatic insects include water boatmen, or backswimmers, water skaters or rovers, and water beetles. Backswimmers are so called because they often turn upside-down and, using their large third pair of legs as oars, swim along. When diving they carry down a store of air trapped between bristles on their body. The skaters skim over the surface of ponds and lakes, using their middle legs like oars and their hind legs to steer. Water beetles live as larvae and adults in fresh water. They stay afloat by keeping a bubble of air under their wing covers. All these aquatic invertebrates are carnivorous, feeding on tadpoles, aquatic worms and small fish.

Insects that scurry across solid surfaces use their legs in a highly coordinated walking action. The legs on each side of the body are moved in sequence from back to front. Cockroaches, for example, when walking slowly move the legs on one side, then on the other.

A millipede runs on more than fifty legs.

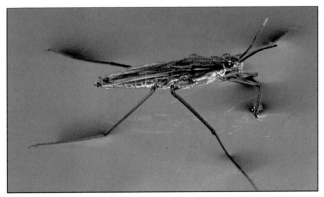

A pond skater walking on water

Offense and defense

Fleas and lice have a tough, leathery skin to prevent injury from the host's scratching. As protection against damage or injury to their wings, members of the beetle family characteristically have elytra. In many ladybirds and cockchafers the elytra are brightly colored to act as a warning to predators, especially birds. Bombardier beetles actively defend themselves by squirting a foul smelling fluid from the end of their abdomen. Similarly many ants squirt formic acid at their enemies, and bees and wasps use their tail sting. Honeybees have a sting equipped with projections, or barbs, so that they cannot pull it out of their attacker and use it again. Bumblebees and wasps can use their sting many times over. Stick and leaf insects resemble the twigs, blades of grass or leaves on which they rest, and tropical tree hoppers are bugs that have bizarre extensions of the thorax believed to function as camouflage. Some caterpillars, the larvae of butterflies and moths, have prickly spines as deterents, and others, such as the puss moth caterpillar, are well camouflaged but when threatened rear up to expose vivid eye spots or facial markings. These frighten off most would-be attackers. Many adult butterflies have eye spots on their wings to deter birds and small mammals, and are also foul tasting. Other butterfly species have, during evolution, acquired similar markings but are pleasant to eat. Because they resemble, or mimic, the nasty-tasting species, they are not eaten as readily.

A stick insect looks just like a twig.

A silkmoth caterpillar has poisonous spines.

An io moth's eye spots frighten attackers.

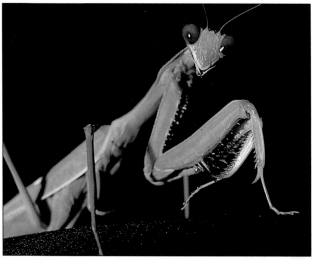

A praying mantis resembles part of a plant.

Feeding

The mouthparts of insects show adaptations to a wide variety of diets. Locusts and leaf insects have mouthparts that can bite and chew plant food. Butterflies and moths have a pair of especially long mouthparts that are joined together by hooks and spines to form a tube, the proboscis, through which the insects suck up nectar. When not in use, the proboscis is coiled up like a clock spring. Bees, too, feed on nectar, and have a special extendible tube that leads from the mouth to a nectar store in the thorax. Houseflies suck up liquid food that usually consists of animal remains. Horseflies, though, use their mouthparts like a sponge to take up blood. Lice and fleas pierce the hosts' skin and suck up blood. Preying mantises have strong chewing mouthparts with which they devour other insects. Aphids feed on the sap of plants but in turn are preyed upon by ladybirds. Hunting wasps live alone and prey mostly on caterpillars. A female paralyzes a caterpillar using her tail sting, drags it to a breeding nest and lays an egg on it. When the larva hatches, it feeds on the caterpillar.

A parasitic wasp lays an egg on a living caterpillar.

A carnivorous dragonfly nymph eating the tadpole of a frog

Senses

An insect's sensory equipment includes a pair of antennae, which can detect sounds and other vibrations, and smells, and a pair of compound eyes. The eyes consist of thousands of identical optical units packed closely together and linked to the brain via nerves. Each unit is made up of a lens-and-cone system that directs light on to a transparent rod, the rhabdom, which is surrounded by light-sensitive nerve cells. When these are stimulated, they send messages to the insect's brain. The units can record the presence or absence of light, its strength, and in some cases, its color, forming a mosaic image.

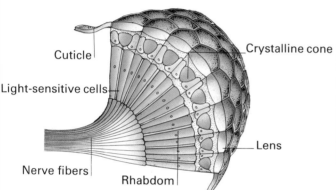

The compound eyes of a deer fly

Parasites

Bugs, fleas and lice are the most common parasitic insects. Many are of economic importance, causing damage to crops and spreading plant and animal diseases, for example the bubonic plague of rats and people. Other parasitic insects include tropical earwigs that live in rats' fur.

Lice live on warm-blooded animals. A host such as a sheep may harbor many thousands of several species. Some pierce the host's skin and suck up blood. Others chew the host's feathers, hair or dead skin cells, but also feed on blood produced by the host's scratching. Fleas have a similar lifestyle to sucking lice. Among bugs, species such as the assassin bugs that are found in all warm places are parasites of other insects, while shield, or stink bugs are serious parasites of plants in semi-tropical regions. Probably the most widespread of the plant-feeding bugs are the sap-feeding aphids.

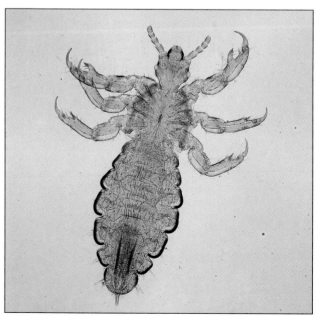

The head louse lives in humans' hair

Mating

Female moths produce chemicals known as pheromones to attract the males (which detect them with their antennae). Among dragonflies and damselflies, the male grasps the female with claspers at the end of his abdomen, then inserts his sperm into her.

Damselflies mating on a blade of grass

Eggs

The success of insects results from the many thousands of eggs females lay each year. Also species such as aphids can reproduce without fertilization of the eggs. In a year, a single aphid could, in ideal conditions, give rise to a population of many billions.

A harlequin bug guarding its eggs

Metamorphosis

Flies, butterflies and mosquitoes have a life cycle typical of highly evolved insects. After mating, the female lays her eggs on or near food suitable for the larvae that will hatch. The larval stage, consisting of a grub or caterpillar, is one in which the insect grows rapidly by continuous feeding. The change, or metamorphosis, of the larva to the adult takes place via a resting stage, the pupa or chrysalis. This is when wings and associated muscles develop and, in butterflies and moths especially, mouthparts change from a leaf-chewing to a nectar-sucking apparatus. During the adult stage, the insects break out of the chrysalis. They disperse to avoid overcrowding, and reproduce, continuing the life cycle.

A red admiral butterfly emerging from its chrysalis

Social life

Bees, wasps, ants and termites are often called social insects because many of them have a lifestyle in which individuals live together in colonies. The colony home of African termites can reach 6m (20ft) tall, and a beehive can contain 100,000 bees. Within a colony there are workers and soldiers, which are specialized to collect food and defend the home, and reproductive males and females. Individuals communicate with each other using chemical signals or, as in honeybees, displays on the honeycomb in the hive. Usually each colony dies out at the end of the year, but not before producing a queen bee and males to fertilize her.

Worker bees on a honeycomb

Weaver ants make a nest of leaves.

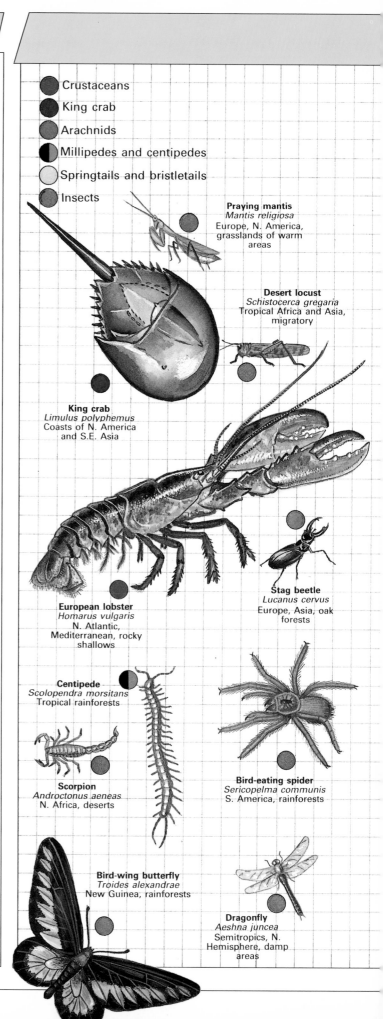

- Crustaceans
- King crab
- Arachnids
- Millipedes and centipedes
- Springtails and bristletails
- Insects

Praying mantis
Mantis religiosa
Europe, N. America, grasslands of warm areas

Desert locust
Schistocerca gregaria
Tropical Africa and Asia, migratory

King crab
Limulus polyphemus
Coasts of N. America and S.E. Asia

Stag beetle
Lucanus cervus
Europe, Asia, oak forests

European lobster
Homarus vulgaris
N. Atlantic, Mediterranean, rocky shallows

Centipede
Scolopendra morsitans
Tropical rainforests

Scorpion
Androctonus aeneas
N. Africa, deserts

Bird-eating spider
Sericopelma communis
S. America, rainforests

Bird-wing butterfly
Troides alexandrae
New Guinea, rainforests

Dragonfly
Aeshna juncea
Semitropics, N. Hemisphere, damp areas

Arthropod chart

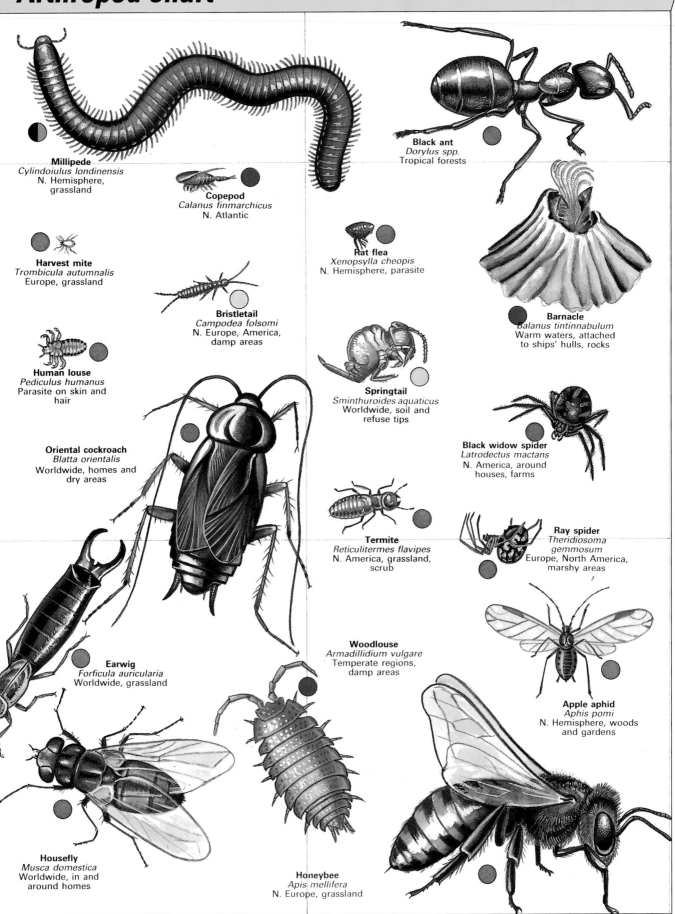

Millipede
Cylindoiulus londinensis
N. Hemisphere,
grassland

Copepod
Calanus finmarchicus
N. Atlantic

Harvest mite
Trombicula autumnalis
Europe, grassland

Bristletail
Campodea folsomi
N. Europe, America,
damp areas

Human louse
Pediculus humanus
Parasite on skin and
hair

Oriental cockroach
Blatta orientalis
Worldwide, homes and
dry areas

Earwig
Forficula auricularia
Worldwide, grassland

Housefly
Musca domestica
Worldwide, in and
around homes

Black ant
Dorylus spp.
Tropical forests

Rat flea
Xenopsylla cheopis
N. Hemisphere, parasite

Barnacle
Balanus tintinnabulum
Warm waters, attached
to ships' hulls, rocks

Springtail
Sminthuroides aquaticus
Worldwide, soil and
refuse tips

Termite
Reticulitermes flavipes
N. America, grassland,
scrub

Black widow spider
Latrodectus mactans
N. America, around
houses, farms

Ray spider
*Theridiosoma
gemmosum*
Europe, North America,
marshy areas

Woodlouse
Armadillidium vulgare
Temperate regions,
damp areas

Apple aphid
Aphis pomi
N. Hemisphere, woods
and gardens

Honeybee
Apis mellifera
N. Europe, grassland

Each square represents 2.5cm (1 inch)

CLASSIFICATION CHART

There are two major divisions within the Animal Kingdom – backboned animals, the vertebrates, which include fish, amphibians and mammals, and animals that lack a backbone, the invertebrates, with which this book deals. The most primitive of the invertebrates, the Protozoans, represent the first type of animals to evolve on Earth more than 3 billion years ago.

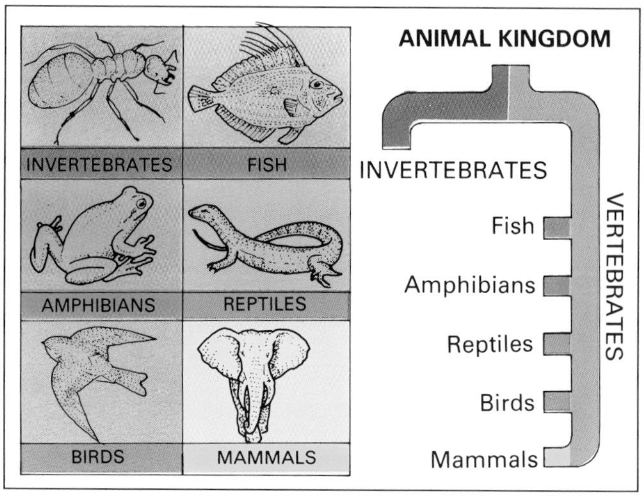

INVERTEBRATES
FISH
AMPHIBIANS
REPTILES
BIRDS
MAMMALS
ANIMAL KINGDOM
INVERTEBRATES
Fish
Amphibians
Reptiles
Birds
Mammals
VERTEBRATES

SEGMENTED WORMS
- Bristleworms
- Earthworms
- Leeches

ARTHROPODS
- Pauropods
- Millipedes
- Centipedes
- Symphylans
- Springtails
- Two-pronged bristletails
- Three-pronged bristletails

ARTHROPODS (continued)
- Insects
  - *Mayflies*
  - *Dragonflies*
  - *Notopterans*
  - *Stoneflies*
  - *Web-spinners*
  - *Cockroaches*
  - *Mantises*
  - *Termites*
  - *Zorapterans*
  - *Grasshoppers*
  - *Stick insects*
  - *Earwigs*
  - *Book-lice*
  - *Bird-lice*
  - *Sucking lice*
  - *Thrips*
  - *Bugs*
  - *Lacewings*
  - *Alderflies*
  - *Snakeflies*
  - *Beetles*
  - *Strepsipterans*
  - *Scorpionflies*
  - *Caddis flies*
  - *Zeuglopterans*
  - *Butterflies and moths*
  - *True flies*
  - *Fleas*
  - *Ants, bees, wasps*
- Arachnids
  - *Scorpions*
  - *Pseudoscorpions*
  - *Camel spiders*
  - *Micro-whip scorpions*
  - *Whip scorpions*
  - *Amblypygids*
  - *Spiders*
  - *Ricinuleids*
  - *Harvestmen*
  - *Mites and ticks*
- Crustaceans
  - *Cephalocarids*
  - *Branchiopods*
  - *Mussel shrimps*
  - *Copepods*
  - *Mystacocarids*
  - *Fish lice*
  - *Barnacles*
  - *Prawns, crabs, lobsters*
- King crabs
- Velvet worms
- Proturans

SPONGES
- Calcareous sponges
- Glass sponges
- Horny sponges

FLATWORMS
- Free-living
- Flukes
- Tapeworms

HEMICHORDATES
- Acorn worms
- Pterobranchs

COELENTERATES
- Hydrozoans
- Jellyfish
- Sea anemones and corals

PROTOZOA
- Flagellates
- Sarcodines
- Spore-formers
- Ciliates

BEARD BEARERS

SEA SPIDERS

ECHINODERMS
- Starfish
- Brittlestars
- Sea urchins
- Sea cucumbers
- Sea lilies

MOLLUSCS
- Monoplacophorans
- Chitons
- Snails and slugs
- Tusk shells
- Bivalve molluscs
- Squid, cuttlefish, octopuses

ASCHELMINTHES
- Rotifers
- Gastrotrichs
- Kinorhynchs
- Priapulids
- Horsehair worms
- Roundworms

MESOZOANS

COMB JELLIES

RIBBON WORMS

ENTOPROCTS

THORNY-HEADED WORMS

PHORONID WORMS

MOSS ANIMALS

LAMP SHELLS

PEANUT WORMS

ECHIUROID WORMS

TONGUE WORMS

WATER BEARS

ARROW WORMS

N.B. Tunicates, such as sea squirts and lancelets, form a link between vertebrates and invertebrates.

GLOSSARY

aquatic animal or plant that lives in water.

asexual reproduction method of producing offspring that does not involve the joining of a male's sperm and female's egg, as in binary fission – the simple division of the animal into two identical individuals – or budding – in which a bud or offshoot develops into a new individual.

brain the coordination and control center of an animal's nervous system.

budding see asexual reproduction.

carnivore meat-eating animal.

cell the smallest unit or building block of living things.

cephalothorax the front part of some arthropods, consisting of the head and thorax sections joined together.

cilia tiny hairs covering the cell surface of some protozoans and other invertebrates, used for feeding or movement.

crustaceans arthropods with a tough exoskeleton armor, a cephalothorax and paired limbs or appendages on all body segments; for example crabs, lobsters, crayfish, prawns.

deoxygenated blood blood low in oxygen but high in carbon dioxide content. Carbon dioxide is a waste product of cell chemistry and must be eliminated from the body.

egg female reproductive cell with its own provision of food for the growing embryo. The egg must usually be fertilized by the male sperm before development of the embryo can begin.

embryo stage in the development of an animal – from the female's fertilized egg until the young hatches.

evolution very slow, probably gradual process by which new species arise as a result of changes (adaptations) that occur in populations of animals or plants.

exoskeleton hard outer covering of arthropods that functions as an external skeleton.

fertilization the fusing together of male and female reproductive cells (sperm and egg) to form an embryo.

habitat place where an animal or plant lives, such as a forest, desert or sea.

hermaphrodite animal with both male and female reproductive organs.

host animal or plant on which a parasite depends for its source of food.

invertebrate animal that lacks a backbone. Many invertebrates are aquatic creatures, including jellyfish, sponges and corals, but insects form the majority.

larva young, immature stage in the life cycles of many animals. It is usually very different in appearance from the adult and cannot reproduce.

mature describing the stage at which animal is sufficiently well developed to be able to reproduce.

nervous system, nerves special body structure(s) able to send, receive and, as the brain, interpret information in the form of electrical messages (known as nerve impulses).

organ major part of an animal or plant which has a specific job, for instance the heart, brain and lungs. Organs are made up of different types of tissues, which are themselves composed of various cells.

oxygenated blood blood rich in oxygen.

parasite organism that lives in or on another one (the host) from which it gets its food. A parasite may eventually kill its food source but it is in its interests not to do so.

parthenogenesis form of reproduction in which the female can produce offspring without fertilization of her eggs. Also known as virgin birth.

plankton tiny animals and plants that float in surface waters of seas, lakes and ponds and form the main food of many larger animals; they include the larvae of many invertebrates.

predator animal that gets its food by hunting and killing other animals.

primitive animal that resembles its distant ancestors, not necessarily one that is simple in structure or undeveloped.

reproduction process of producing offspring. It usually involves the male fertilizing the female's egg with his sperm (sexual reproduction), although many primitive animals can reproduce by asexual means.

scavenger animal that eats dead or dying animals.

species animals and plants that have the same structure and that are capable of reproducing together.

sperm the male's reproductive cells. In sexual reproduction sperm must fertilize the female's eggs for offspring to be produced.

vertebral column another name for the backbone. It consists of many bony units linked together to form a flexible stiffening rod the length of the body.

INDEX

All entries in bold are found in the Glossary

Photographic Credits
(l=left, r=right, t=top, b=bottom, c=center)
Cover and pages 9 (t and b), 21 (t), 24 (b): Ardea; contents page: David George/Planet Earth; pages 7 (t), 8, 14 (b), 15 (t), 20 (r), 21 (b), 22 (both), 23 (t), 24 (t and r), 25 (t), 27 (t and b), 28 (tl and tr), 29 (both), 30 (both), 31 (l and b) and back cover: Bruce Colman; page 7 (b) and 10 (t): Christian Petron/Planet Earth; page 9 (c): Science Photo Library; pages 10 (l) and 28 (bl): Planet Earth; page 10 (r): Peter Scoones/Planet Earth; page 11: Robert Arnold/Planet Earth; pages 14 (t) and 32 (b): Survival Anglia; page 15 (b): Bill Wood/Planet Earth; page 16 (t): Carl Roessler/Planet Earth; pages 16 (l), 25 (b) and 27 (l): Ken Lucas/Planet Earth; page 16 (r): Mike Laverick/Planet Earth; page 20 (l): Peter David/Planet Earth; pages 23 (b), 31 (r) and 32 (t): David Maitland/Planet Earth; page 29 (br): Peter Stephenson/Planet Earth.